Taylor

by Iain Gray

LangSyne
PUBLISHING
WRITING *to* REMEMBER

Lang**Syne**

PUBLISHING

WRITING *to* REMEMBER

79 Main Street, Newtongrange,
Midlothian EH22 4NA
Tel: 0131 344 0414   Fax: 0845 075 6085
E-mail: info@lang-syne.co.uk
www.langsyneshop.co.uk

Design by Dorothy Meikle
Printed by Printwell Ltd
© Lang Syne Publishers Ltd 2017

ISBN 978-1-85217-600-6

Taylor

MOTTO:
He obtains whatever he seeks
(or)
He accomplishes whatever he undertakes.

CREST:
A naked arm with the
fist grasping an arrow.

NAME variations include:
Tailer
Tailler
Tailor

Chapter one:

The origins of popular surnames

by George Forbes and Iain Gray

***If you don't know where you came from, you won't know where you're going** is a frequently quoted observation and one that has a particular resonance today when there has been a marked upsurge in interest in genealogy, with increasing numbers of people curious to trace their family roots.*

Main sources for genealogical research include census returns and official records of births, marriages and deaths – and the key to unlocking the detail they contain is obviously a family surname, one that has been 'inherited' and passed from generation to generation.

No matter our station in life, we all have a surname – but it was not until about the middle of the fourteenth century that the practice of being identified by a particular surname became commonly established throughout the British Isles.

Previous to this, it was normal for a person to be identified through the use of only a forename.

But as population gradually increased and there were many more people with the same forename, surnames were adopted to distinguish one person, or community, from another.

Many common English surnames are patronymic in origin, meaning they stem from the forename of one's father – with 'Johnson,' for example, indicating 'son of John.'

It was the Normans, in the wake of their eleventh century conquest of Anglo-Saxon England, a pivotal moment in the nation's history, who first brought surnames into usage – although it was a gradual process.

For the Normans, these were names initially based on the title of their estates, local villages and chateaux in France to distinguish and identify these landholdings.

Such grand descriptions also helped enhance the prestige of these warlords and generally glorify their lofty positions high above the humble serfs slaving away below in the pecking order who had only single names, often with Biblical connotations as in Pierre and Jacques.

The only descriptive distinctions among the peasantry concerned their occupations, like 'Pierre the swineherd' or 'Jacques the ferryman.'

Roots of surnames that came into usage in England not only included Norman-French, but also Old French, Old Norse, Old English, Middle English, German, Latin, Greek, Hebrew and the Gaelic languages of the Celts.

The Normans themselves were originally Vikings, or 'Northmen', who raided, colonised and eventually settled down around the French coastline.

The had sailed up the Seine in their longboats in 900AD under their ferocious leader Rollo and ruled the roost in north eastern France before sailing over to conquer England in 1066 under Duke William of Normandy – better known to posterity as William the Conqueror, or King William I of England.

Granted lands in the newly-conquered England, some of their descendants later acquired territories in Wales, Scotland and Ireland – taking not only their own surnames, but also the practice of adopting a surname, with them.

But it was in England where Norman rule and custom first impacted, particularly in relation to the adoption of surnames.

This is reflected in the famous *Domesday Book*, a massive survey of much of England and Wales, ordered by William I, to determine who owned what, what it was worth and therefore how much they were liable to pay in taxes to the voracious Royal Exchequer.

Completed in 1086 and now held in the National Archives in Kew, London, 'Domesday' was an Old English word meaning 'Day of Judgement.'

This was because, in the words of one contemporary chronicler, "its decisions, like those of the Last Judgement, are unalterable."

It had been a requirement of all those English landholders – from the richest to the poorest – that they identify themselves for the purposes of the survey and for future reference by means of a surname.

This is why the *Domesday Book*, although written in Latin as was the practice for several centuries with both civic and ecclesiastical records, is an invaluable source for the early appearance of a wide range of English surnames.

Several of these names were coined in connection with occupations.

These include Baker and Smith, while Cooks, Chamberlains, Constables and Porters were to be found carrying out duties in large medieval households.

The church's influence can be found in names such as Bishop, Friar and Monk while the popular name of Bennett derives from the late fifth to mid-sixth century Saint Benedict, founder of the Benedictine order of monks.

The early medical profession is represented by Barber, while businessmen produced names that include Merchant and Sellers.

Down at the village watermill, the names that cropped up included Millar/Miller, Walker and Fuller, while other self-explanatory trades included Cooper, Tailor, Mason and Wright.

Even the scenery was utilised as in Moor, Hill, Wood and Forrest – while the hunt and the chase supplied names that include Hunter, Falconer, Fowler and Fox.

Colours are also a source of popular surnames, as in Black, Brown, Gray/Grey, Green and White, and would have denoted the colour of the clothing the person habitually wore or, apart from the obvious exception of 'Green', one's hair colouring or even complexion.

The surname Red developed into Reid, while

Blue was rare and no-one wanted to be associated with yellow.

Rather self-important individuals took surnames that include Goodman and Wiseman, while physical attributes crept into surnames such as Small and Little.

Many families proudly boast the heraldic device known as a Coat of Arms, as featured on our front cover.

The central motif of the Coat of Arms would originally have been what was borne on the shield of a warrior to distinguish himself from others on the battlefield.

Not featured on the Coat of Arms, but highlighted on page three, is the family motto and related crest – with the latter frequently different from the central motif.

Adding further variety to the rich cultural heritage that is represented by surnames is the appearance in recent times in lists of the 100 most common names found in England of ones that include Khan, Patel and Singh – names that have proud roots in the vast sub-continent of India.

Echoes of a far distant past can still be found in our surnames and they can be borne with pride in commemoration of our forebears.

Chapter two:

Royal favour

Ranked 4th in some lists of the 100 most popular surnames found in England today, 'Taylor' is an occupational name derived from the Old French 'tailleur', meaning 'cutter', and indicating someone who worked with cloth – 'cutting' it to fashion garments.

'Tailleir', in turn, derives from the Latin 'taliator', meaning 'to cut'.

By the very nature of the occupation of dealing with cloth, the name is of very early genesis but, in common with many others found today, it was popularised in the wake of the Norman Conquest of 1066.

By this date England had become a nation with several powerful competitors to the throne.

In what were extremely complex family, political and military machinations, the monarch was Harold II, who had succeeded to the throne following the death of Edward the Confessor.

But his right to the throne was contested by two powerful competitors – his brother-in-law King

Harold Hardrada of Norway, in alliance with Tostig, Harold II's brother, and Duke William II of Normandy.

In what has become known as The Year of Three Battles, Hardrada invaded England and gained victory over the English king on September 20 at the battle of Fulford, in Yorkshire.

Five days later, however, Harold II decisively defeated his brother-in-law and brother at the battle of Stamford Bridge.

But he had little time to celebrate his victory, having to immediately march south from Yorkshire to encounter a mighty invasion force, led by Duke William, that had landed at Hastings, in East Sussex.

Harold's battle-hardened but exhausted force of Anglo-Saxon soldiers confronted the Normans on October 14 in a battle subsequently depicted on the Bayeux tapestry – a 23ft. long strip of embroidered linen thought to have been commissioned eleven years after the event by the Norman Odo of Bayeux.

Harold drew up a strong defensive position, at the top of Senlac Hill, building a shield wall to repel Duke William's cavalry and infantry.

The Normans suffered heavy losses, but through a combination of the deadly skill of their archers and the ferocious determination of their cavalry they eventually won the day.

Anglo-Saxon morale had collapsed on the battlefield as word spread through the ranks that Harold had been killed – the Bayeux Tapestry depicting this as having happened when he was struck by an arrow to the head.

Amidst the carnage of the battlefield, it was difficult to identify him – the last of the Anglo-Saxon kings.

Some sources assert William ordered his body to be thrown into the sea, while others state it was secretly buried at Waltham Abbey.

What is known with certainty is that William, in celebration of his great victory, founded Battle Abbey, near the site of the battle, ordering that the altar be sited on the spot where Harold was believed to have fallen.

William was declared King of England on December 25, and the complete subjugation of his Anglo-Saxon subjects followed.

Those Normans who had fought on his behalf were rewarded with the lands of Anglo-Saxons, many of whom sought exile abroad as mercenaries.

Within an astonishingly short space of time,

Norman manners, customs and law were imposed on England – laying the basis for what subsequently became established 'English' custom and practice.

A William de Taillur is recorded in Somerset in 1182, but it is the county of Kent with which bearers of the name came to be particularly associated.

Of Anglo-Norman roots, a John Taylefer, or Taylor, is recorded as having been a knight in the service of Edward III – an indication of the high status some early bearers of the name had achieved.

Born in about 1324 at Shadoxhurst, Ashford, in Kent, he died in 1377 – the same year as his monarch.

While John Taylor achieved high honours and distinction as a trusted member of the royal establishment, others of the Taylor name were decidedly less well favoured.

A theologian and priest, William Taylor was a follower of the religious teachings of John Wycliffe, the fourteenth century theologian and radical philosopher who, rejecting Papal authority and the right of clergy to own property, was the guiding light behind what became known as the Lollard movement.

Lollards, such as Taylor, were perceived as a dangerous threat to the established order and were accordingly persecuted.

Details of Taylor's early life are not known, although it is known that in about 1405 he was principal of St Edmond Hall, Oxford, and that he argued vociferously for the Lollard cause.

Arrested, condemned for his 'heretical' beliefs and stripped of his status as a priest, he was subjected to the horrific ordeal in March of 1423 of being burned alive at Smithfield, London, in front of a baying mob.

Holding high office during the reign of Henry VIII, John Taylor was the English priest and civil servant born in about 1480.

A triplet, his family appears to have been well connected in royal circles, because it is known that Henry VII met him and his two brothers in their childhood and took upon himself the responsibility for their education.

In a much later century, this act inspired what is known as Queen Victoria's Royal Bounty for Triplets – a cash gift for the benefit of triplets 'in necessitous circumstances.'

Taylor served as one of the royal chaplains at the funeral of Henry VII in 1509 and was appointed clerk and chaplain to his successor Henry VIII.

One of his duties was to act as one of the

commissioners to decide whether or not the king's marriage to Catherine of Aragon was valid.

Henry, anxious to divorce his queen in order to marry Anne Boleyn, had sought to persuade the Papal authorities that, because Catherine was the widow of his elder brother Arthur, the marriage could not be regarded as valid.

He was unsuccessful, but this did not prevent him divorcing Catherine and marrying Anne.

Appointed Archdeacon of Derby in 1515 and then Royal Ambassador to Burgundy and France, Taylor was one of the chaplains who attended Henry in June of 1520 at the glittering ceremonials that took place on the colourfully name *Camp du Drap d'Or – Field of the Cloth of Gold* – near Calais.

Featuring tournaments with the cream of English and French knighthood, the ceremonials had been arranged to further seal a bond of amity between Henry and King Francis I of France.

Appointed Archdeacon of Halifax in 1528, Taylor also served, from 1527 until his death in 1534, as Master of the Rolls of the Court of Chancery – in charge of the civil division of the Court of Appeal.

Chapter three:

Inventive minds

Bearers of the Taylor name have left an indelible mark on the historical record through endeavours and pursuits that range from the sciences to the worlds of invention and politics.

Born in 1685 in Middlesex, Brook Taylor was the English mathematician who devised what are now known as Taylor's Theorem and the Taylor Series.

In the bafflingly abstract and complex world of higher mathematics – at least to a lay person – he is considered as having 'laid the main foundation of differential calculus.'

Among the applications of his theorem, was the ability to use it to determine the movement of a vibrating string.

A Fellow of the prestigious scientific think-tank the Royal Society, he died in 1731.

In the equally abstract realms of philosophy, Alfred Taylor, born in 1869 in Oundle, East Midlands, was the leading British philosopher who wrote works on metaphysics and the philosophies of religion and morals.

Influenced by the works of the ancient Greek philosopher Plato and considered one of the greatest English Platonists of his time, he died in 1945, while his many works include his 1926 *Plato: The Man and His Work*.

In contemporary times, Charles Taylor, born in Montreal in 1931, is the Canadian philosopher who, in recognition of his contribution to the philosophy of social science, intellectual history and political philosophy, was made a Companion of the Order of Canada in 1995.

To the world of invention and in Scotland, a common sight on the River Clyde at one time were the many gaily decorated paddle steamers that annually took Glaswegians 'doon the watter' for holiday excursions to resorts such as Rothesay.

These holidaymakers owed a debt to James Taylor, born in the tiny village of Leadhills, in Lanarkshire, in 1758, and who is now recognised as pioneering the first practical application of steam power to vessels.

Educated at Wallacehall School, in Closeburn, Dumfriesshire, and Edinburgh University, Taylor was a man of many interests that ranged from geology and mineralogy to chemistry and mechanics.

He trained as a doctor, but in 1785 he was employed as a tutor to the family of the wealthy Patrick Miller, of Dalswinton, in Dumfriesshire.

This would prove to be a turning point not only in Taylor's career, but also in the history of steam navigation.

Taylor had been a school friend of the inventor and engine builder William Symington, and, with Patrick Miller's active encouragement, the pair built a paddleboat powered with a steam engine.

Its first trial was on Dalswinton Loch, on October 14, 1788, when it reached the then remarkable speed on water of 5mph, and one tradition relates that Scotland's national bard, Robert Burns, was one of the excited passengers.

The experiment was later repeated on the Forth and Clyde Canal, the paddleboat achieving the dizzying speed of 7mph. From such small beginnings, however, Taylor, who died in 1825, had laid the blueprints for the great paddle steamers of the future.

Taking to the skies, Charles Edward Taylor was the aviation engineer who constructed the first aircraft engine used by the brothers Orville and Wilbur Wright, the American aviators who made the world's first controlled, powered and heavier-than-air human flight on December 17, 1903.

This was at Kitty Hawk, North Carolina, when an aircraft made from machinery and other materials cobbled together in their workshop originally used to repair bicycles, took to the air.

The rudimentary machine was later perfected as the Wright Flyer I, and the brothers went on to invent aircraft controls that made fixed wing flight possible.

Born in 1868, Taylor was first employed by the brothers to help out in their business of repairing bicycles.

But with both he and the brothers' minds fixed on much higher challenges, Taylor designed and built a special water-cooled aluminium engine.

This engine proved a success, although on a flight demonstration in 1908 before representatives of the U.S. Army of what was known as the 'Military Flyer', at Fort Myer, Virginia, the aircraft crashed because of a faulty propeller.

Orville Wright, who had been piloting the aeroplane, was pulled from the wreckage by Taylor, while U.S. army lieutenant Thomas Selfridge, who had been a passenger, was killed.

Later the Wright Company's leading mechanic, Taylor died in 1956, while the Federal Aviation Administration's (FAA) Charles Taylor Master Mechanic Award is named in his honour.

Still in the skies, Sir Patrick Gordon Taylor was the Australian aviator who, in 1935, was awarded the Empire Gallantry Medal for his death-defying actions during an Australia to New Zealand airmail flight.

The starboard engine of his aircraft had failed and, in an attempt to save himself and his fellow crew, he perilously clambered onto the wing in order to successfully drain oil from a malfunctioning motor and transfer it to another.

Along with navigator Richard Archibold, he made the first flight across the Indian Ocean in 1939 – from Australia to Kenya – while in 1951 he made a South Pacific flight from Australia to Chile, via Tahiti and then on to Easter Island; knighted for his services to aviation, he died in 1966.

Returning to the sciences, Richard Taylor, born in 1929 in Medicine Hat, Alberta, is the Canadian physicist who, in 1990, shared the Nobel Prize for Physics along with Henry Kendall and Jerome Friedman for his work on particle physics.

Appointed a Member of the Companion Order of Canada in 2005, the Stanford University professor is also a member of a number of prestigious scientific bodies that include the American Physical Society, the Royal Society of London and the Canadian Association of Physicists.

In the world of politics, George Taylor, born in Ireland in 1716 and who later immigrated to America, was one of the signatories on July 4, 1776, of the American Declaration of Independence.

Owner of an ironworks that manufactured much-needed arms and ammunition for the American cause during the American Revolutionary War of 1775 to 1783, it was in his capacity as a representative for the state of Pennsylvania that he signed the famous declaration; he died in 1781.

A hero of the Mexican-American War of 1846 to 1848, in which he served in the U.S. Army with the rank of major general, Zachary Taylor later served – from March of 1849 until his death in July of the following year – as 12th President of the United States.

Born in 1784 in Orange County, Virginia to a wealthy plantation-owning family of English ancestry, it was during the Mexican-American War that he distinguished himself at the battles of Palo Alto and Monterey.

Nicknamed "Old Rough and Ready", Taylor, as president, attempted to thwart attempts for the expansion of slavery into New Mexico and California – although he was himself a slave-owner.

This has given rise to conspiracy theories that exist to this day that his death, ostensibly from a stomach complaint, may in fact have been caused by deliberate poisoning – with arsenic being laced into his food through a plot by disgruntled Southern slavers.

Taylor County in Georgia, Taylor County in Iowa and Taylor Highway in Virginia are all named in his honour.

His daughter Sarah, born in 1814, died in 1835 – only three months after marrying Jefferson Davies, who went on to serve during the American Civil War of 1861 to 1865 as President of the Confederate States of America.

His son, Richard Taylor, born in 1826 and who died in 1879, served with the Confederate States Army as a brigade commander in Virginia.

Better known as the great twentieth century British historian A.J.P. Taylor, Alan John Percival Taylor was born in Lancashire in 1906.

A lecturer for a time in modern history at Manchester University, he returned to Oxford University, where he had studied, as a lecturer in international history.

In addition to a career as a lecturer and broadcaster, Taylor, who died in 1990, had the knack of making history accessible to the non-academic.

Accordingly, books such as *The Origins of the Second World War* and *English History 1914-1945* became best sellers.

Chapter four:

On the world stage

An icon of the silver screen, Elizabeth Taylor, more fondly known as Liz Taylor and later more formally known as Dame Elizabeth Taylor, was the British-American actress whose Hollywood film debut came at the tender age of only nine.

Her American parents were living and working in London when she was born there in 1932.

Her father, Francis, was an art dealer while her mother Sara was a former actress, and it was shortly before the outbreak of the Second World War in 1939 that they returned to the United States, settling in Los Angeles.

Her father's art gallery attracted a host of celebrities, including Hollywood film moguls, and it was through this that the future film star came to the attention of the industry.

Struck by the beauty she displayed at even such a young age, with startling violet eyes, she was signed up by Universal Pictures at the age of nine, making her screen debut in *One Born Every Minute*.

Switching from Universal to MGM, the child

actress was cast in the 1943 *Lassie Come Home*, while other screen credits throughout the 1940s include the 1944 *National Velvet*, the 1946 *Courage of Lassie* and, from 1949, *Little Women*.

The latter film was her last adolescent role, and she went on to star in a range of films that include the 1950 *Father of the Bride*, the 1956 *Giant*, starring beside James Dean, the 1959 *Suddenly Last Summer* and, from 1960, *Butterfield 8*, for which she won an Academy Award for Best Actress.

A second Academy Award, for Best Actress in a Leading Role, came in 1966 for her performance as Martha in *Who's Afraid of Virginia Woolf?*

Also famed for her glamorous lifestyle, she was married eight times to seven husbands – the most famous being the Welsh actor Richard Burton.

The couple, who had a tempestuous relationship and who starred together in six films that include the 1965 *The Sandpiper* and the 1967 *The Taming of the Shrew*, were first married from 1964 to 1974 and then from 1975 to 1976.

Burton had been her fifth husband, having previously been married and divorced from the American socialite and hotel heir Conrad "Nicky" Hilton, the actor Michael Wilding, Hollywood producer Mike Todd, singer Eddie Fisher, and the Republican politician John Warner.

Following her final divorce from Burton, she was married and then divorced from construction worker Larry Fortensky – the marriage ceremony taking place in 1996 at her friend Michael Jackson's Neverland Ranch.

A champion of AIDS and HIV programmes, in 1985 she co-founded the American Foundation for AIDS research and, eight years later, the Elizabeth Taylor AIDS Foundation.

Appointed a Dame Commander of the Order of the British Empire (DBE) in 1999, she quipped: "I've always been a broad, now I'm a dame!"

She died in 2001, the recipient of many other honours and awards that include a Presidential Citizens Medal for her humanitarian work, lifetime achievement awards from both the American Film Institute and the Screen Actors Guild and a star on the Hollywood Walk of Fame.

Also the recipient of a star on the Hollywood Walk of Fame, Spangler Arlington Brugh was the American actor of film and television better known by his stage name of **Robert Taylor**.

Born in 1911 in Filley, Nebraska, it was

while appearing in a stage production of *Journey's End* that he was spotted by a talent scout for MGM.

His screen debut came two years later in *Handy Andy*, going on to star in films that include, opposite Greta Garbo, the 1936 *Camille*, the 1941 *Billy the Kid*, the 1942 *Johnny Eager*, opposite Lana Turner and, from 1943, *Baatan*.

Nicknamed "The Man with the Perfect Profile", other major film credits including the 1949 *Conspirator*, the 1950 *Quo Vadis* and, with his then wife Barbara Stanwyck, the 1964 *Nightwalker*.

Taylor died in 1969.

Born in 1930 in Lidcombe, Sydney, Rodney Sturt Taylor is the Australian actor better known as **Rod Taylor**.

Working for a time as a commercial artist, he took to the stage and went on to star in films that include the 1957 *Raintree County*, the 1960 *The Time Machine*, director Alfred Hitchcock's 1963 *The Birds* and the 1970 *Forever Amber* – while in 2009 he came out of retirement for the role of Winston Churchill in Quentin Tarantino's *Inglourious Basterds*.

On British television screens, **Gwen Taylor**, born in 1939 in Derby, is the English actress whose many credits include *Murder Most Horrid*, *Yes, Prime*

Minister, *Inspector Morse*, *Midsomer Murders*, *Duty Free* and *Coronation Street*.

Best known as a member, along with Bill Oddie and Graeme Garden, of the cast of the television comedy series *The Goodies*, Timothy Julian Brooke-Taylor is the English comic actor better known as **Tim Brooke-Taylor**.

Born in 1940 in Buxton, Derbyshire, and the recipient of an OBE for his services to entertainment, he is also known for work on radio as a panellist on shows that include *I'm Sorry, I'll Read That Again* and *I'm Sorry, I Haven't a Clue*.

Bearers of the Taylor name have also excelled in the highly competitive world of sport.

Born in 1978 in Albany, Georgia, **Angelo F. Taylor** is the American track and field athlete who won the gold medal in the 400-metres hurdles at both the 2000 and 2008 Olympics. World champion with the U.S. team in the 4x400-metres relay in 2007, 2009 and 2011, he was a silver medallist in the event at the 2012 Olympics in London.

From athletics to darts, Philip Douglas Taylor, better known as **Phil Taylor**, is the English professional player who has, to date, won sixteen World Championships.

Born in 1960 in Burslem, Stoke-on-Trent and nicknamed "The Power", he was runner-up in 2006 and 2010 for the accolade of BBC Sports Personality of the Year.

On the snooker table, **Dennis Taylor**, born in 1949 in Coalisland, Co. Tyrone, is the Northern Irish retired player who won the 1985 World Championship and, two years later, the Masters; he is now a popular commentator on the game for the BBC.

Also on the green baize of the snooker table, **David Taylor**, born in 1943 in Bowdon, Cheshire is the English semi-retired player who won both the English and the World Amateur Championships in 1968.

Bearers of the Taylor name are particularly prominent in the creative world of music.

Born in 1948 in Massachusetts General Hospital, where his father Isaac M. Taylor was then a resident physician, James Vernon Taylor is the multi-award-winning American singer, songwriter and guitarist better known as **James Taylor**.

Of Scots ancestry through his father, his mother Gertrude, née Woodward, studied at the New England Conservatory of Music and pursued a career as an opera singer before her marriage.

The family moved to North Carolina when Taylor was aged three and his father took up the post of assistant professor of medicine at the University of North Carolina School of Medicine.

Learning to play the cello as a child and later the guitar, his first major hit was *Fire and Rain*, the song that in 1972 earned him a Grammy Award for Best Pop Vocal Performance (Male).

Other Grammy awards in the same category are for the singles *You've Got a Friend*, *Handy Man* and *Don't Let Me Be Lonely Tonight*. Yet another Grammy Award, for Best Pop Album, came in 2001 for *Hourglass*.

Married for a time to fellow singer and songwriter Carly Simon, his many honours and awards include induction into the Rock and Roll Hall of Fame and the Songwriters Hall of Fame, while he is ranked 84th in *Rolling Stone* magazine's list of "The Immortals: 100 Greatest Artists of All Time."

In a different musical genre another James Taylor – **J. T. Taylor** – is the American singer and actor better known as the former lead singer of the rhythm and blues and funk band Kool and the Gang.

Born in 1953 in Laurens, South Carolina and

a former schoolteacher, he co-wrote top albums that include *Ladies Night* and *Celebrate!*

A session bass guitarist for bands and artistes that included The Monkees and Jerry Lee Lewis, **Larry Taylor**, born in 1942 in New York City, is best known for having been, since 1967, a member of the band Canned Heat.

Best known for his 1970 internationally top-selling hit *Indiana Wants Me*, Richard Dean Taylor is the Canadian singer, songwriter and record producer better known as **R. Dean Taylor**.

A record producer for Motown Records during the 1960s and 1970s, he is also known for other hits that include *Gotta See Jane*.

Voted the eighth greatest drummer in classic rock music history in a poll conducted by Planet Rock Radio, Roger Meddows Taylor is the drummer with British rock band Queen better known as **Roger Taylor**.

Born in 1949 in King's Lynn, Norfolk, as a songwriter he wrote a number of the band's hits that include *Radio Ga Ga*, *A Kind of Magic* and *These are the Days of our Lives*.

Although not related, no fewer than three bearers of the Taylor name – along with vocalist

Simon Le Bon and keyboard player Nick Rhodes–have been members of the British new wave band Duran Duran, whose best-selling singles include the 1981 *Girls on Film*, *Rio* and *Wild Boys*.

Born in Birmingham in 1960, **John Taylor**, a founder member of the band, plays bass guitar while **Roger Taylor**, born in the same city in 1960, is the drummer; the third Taylor is guitarist **Andy Taylor**, born in 1961 in Cullercoats, Tyne and Wear.

Although her name is unfortunately relatively unknown today, **Jane Taylor** nevertheless has left an enduring legacy in the form of the famous nursery rhyme *Twinkle, Twinkle, Little Star*.

Born into a literary family in Lavenham, Suffolk, in 1783, she and her sister Ann both wrote poetry, and some of their collected work was published in 1805 as *Rhymes for the Nursery*.

It was Jane who penned *The Star* which, later put to a French tune, became what is now *Twinkle, Twinkle, Little Star*.

She died in 1824, while the house where she lived with her family – Shilling Grange, in Shilling Street, Lavenham, and where she wrote the internationally beloved rhyme, can still be seen to this day.